The Joy of Children's Favorites

W9-BNZ-856

**Best loved songs, nursery rhymes, play tunes, and singing games.
Easy piano arrangements with words and chord names.
by Denes Agay, with activities by Joy Yelin and illustrations by Janice Fried.**

Yorktown Music Press, Inc.
New York/London/Sydney/Cologne

International Standard Book Number: 0.8256.8074.3

Exclusive Distributors:
Music Sales Corporation
225 Park Avenue South, New York, NY 10003 USA
Music Sales Limited
8/9 Frith Street, London W1V 5TZ England
Music Sales Pty. Limited
120 Rothschild Street, Rosebery, Sydney, NSW 2018, Australia

Printed in the United States of America by
Vicks Lithograph and Printing Corporation

Contents

Bingo

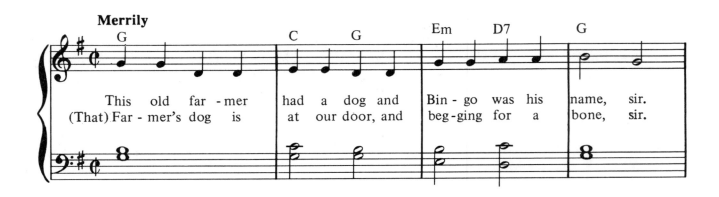

Merrily

G	C G	Em D7 G

This old far - mer / had a dog and / Bin - go was his / name, sir.
(That) Far - mer's dog is / at our door, and / beg-ging for a / bone, sir.

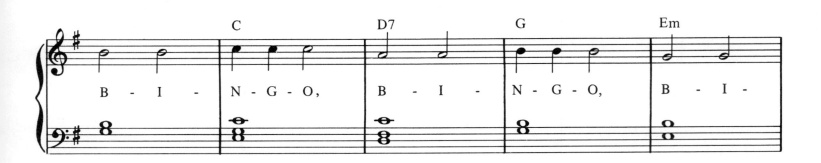

C	D7	G	Em

B - I - / N - G-O, / B - I - / N - G-O, / B - I -

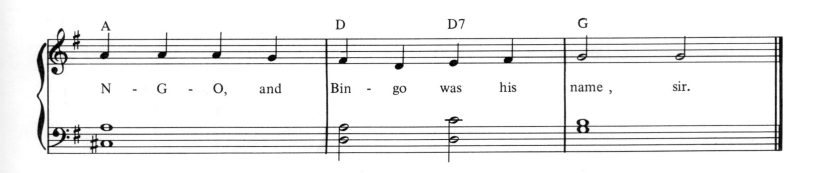

A	D D7	G

N - G - O, and / Bin - go was his / name, sir.

Hot Cross Buns

Lively

Hot cross buns, Hot cross buns, One a pen-ny, two a pen-ny,

Hot cross buns. If you have no daugh-ters, Give them to your sons,

One a pen-ny, two a pen-ny, Hot cross buns.

Jack and Jill

Gaily

Jack and Jill went up the hill to fetch a pail of wa - ter;

Jack fell down and broke his crown, and Jill came tum - bling af - ter.

2. Up Jack got and home did trot
   As fast as he could caper;
   Went to bed to mend his head
   With vinegar and brown paper.

3. Jill came in, how she did grin
   To see Jack's paper plaster;
   Mother, vexed, did whip her next
   For causing Jack's disaster.

Sing a Song of Sixpence

Merrily

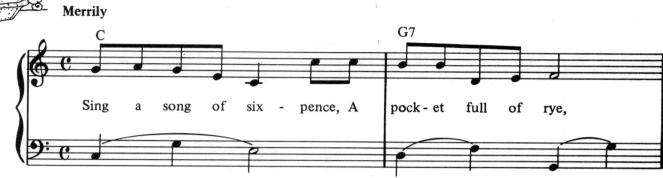

C ... G7

Sing a song of six - pence, A pock - et full of rye,

C

Four and twen - ty black - birds Baked in a pie. When the pie was o - pened, The

G ... A Dm ... G7 C

birds be - gan to sing; was - n't that a dain - ty dish to set be-fore the king?

I'm a Little Teapot

Comfortably

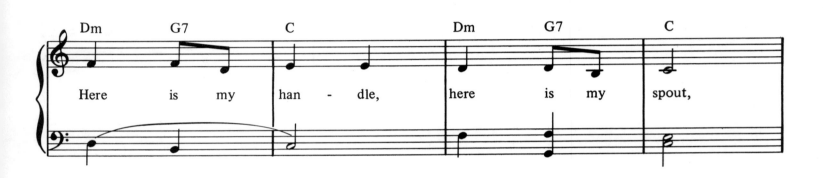

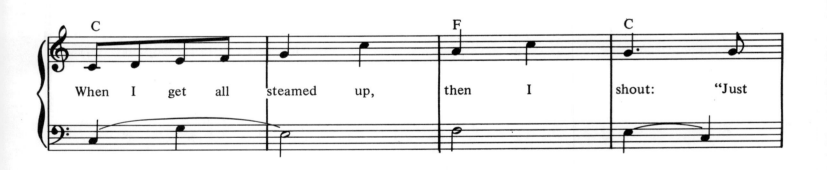

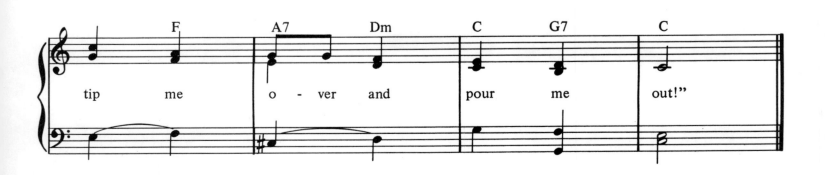

The Train Song

Quite fast

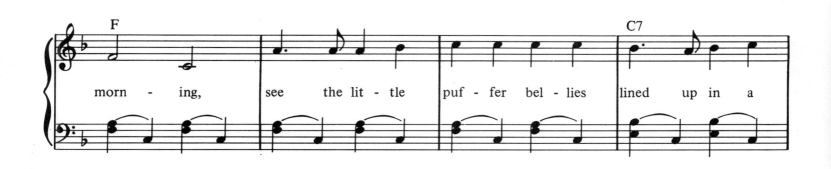

If You're Happy and You Know It

Here We Go 'round the Mulberry Bush

Lazy Mary, Will You Get Up?

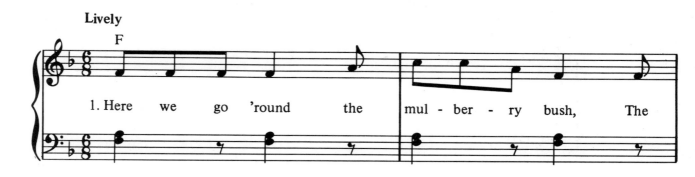

This is a good one for activity. Just follow the actions suggested by the words.

2. This is the way we *clap* our hands,
　　　　　Clap our hands, clap our hands,
　This is the way we clap our hands
　　　　　On a cold and frosty morning.

3. This is the way we *stamp* our feet, *etc.*

4. This is the way we *wash* our clothes,

5. This is the way we *iron* our clothes,

6. This is the way we *sweep* the floor,

The same tune with different words: "Lazy Mary, Will You Get Up?"

1. Lazy Mary, will you get up?
　　　Will you get up, will you get up?
　Lazy Mary, will you get up
　　　This cold and frosty morning?

　No, Mother, I won't get up,
　　　I won't get, I won't get up;
　No, Mother, I won't get up
　　　This cold and frosty morning.

2. What if I give you some bread and jam? *etc.*

　No, Mother, I won't get up, *etc.*

3. What if I give you some bacon and egg?

　No, Mother, I won't get up,

4. What if I give you a crack on the head?

　YES, Mother, I will get up,

We Sail and We Sail and We Stop!

Lively

mf We sail and we sail and we stop! We sail and we sail and we stop! We sail and we sail and we sail and we sail and we sail and we sail and we stop!

Baa! Baa! Black Sheep

Moderately

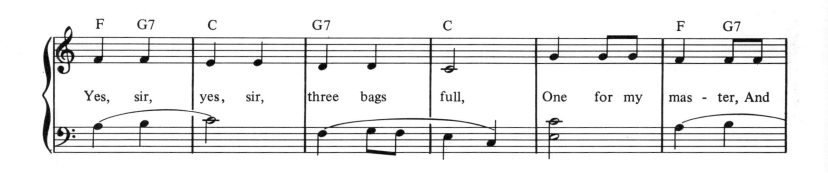

Baa, baa, black sheep, have you an-y wool?

Yes, sir, yes, sir, three bags full, One for my mas-ter, And one for my dame, And one for the lit-tle boy who lives down the

lane.

What Shall We Do when We All Go Out?

1. What shall we do when we all go out, All go out, all go out; What shall we do when we all go out, when we all go out to play?

This song has the action built right in!

2. We will *climb* an apple tree,
       Apple tree, apple tree.
   We will climb an apple tree
       When we all go out to play.

3. We will *jump* like jumping jacks, *etc.*

4. We will *catch* some lightning bugs,

5. We will *ride** our bikes around,

*Lie down on the floor on your back and "pedal" with your feet in the air.

Little Tommy Tucker

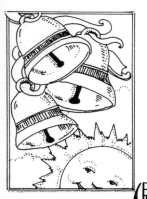

Are You Sleeping, Brother John?

Frère Jacques

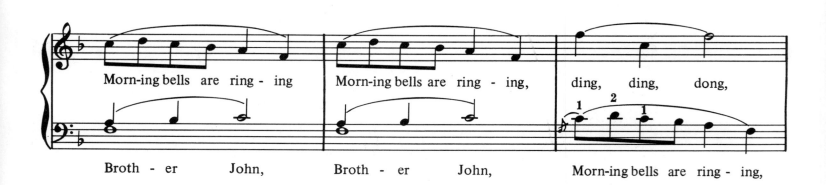

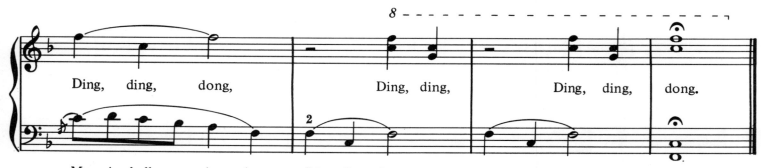

Frère Jacques, Frère Jacques,
    Dormez vous? Dormez vous?
Sonnez les matines, sonnez les matines.
    Din, din, don. Din, din, don.

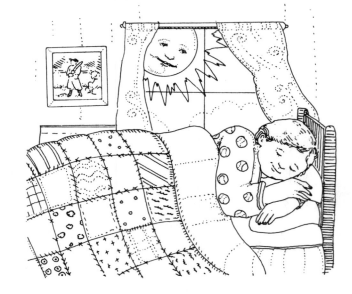

Where Is Thumbkin?

to the tune of "Are You Sleeping, Brother John?"

Where is Thumbkin? Where is Thumbkin?
Here I am, here I am.

How are you this morning?
    Very well, I thank you.
Run and hide,
    run and hide.

Hide both hands behind your back.
Bring out one hand in front of you, holding up your thumb and tucking the other fingers into a fist.
Wiggle one thumb.
Wiggle the other thumb.
Quickly "run and hide" one thumb behind you.
"Run and hide" the other thumb.

Repeat the lyrics and actions holding up each finger in turn:

Where is pointer? *etc.*

Where is tall man?

Where is ring man?

Where is pinky?

The final verse:

Where's the whole family? Where's the whole family?
    Here we are, here we are.
How are you this morning? Very well, we thank you.
    Run and hide, run and hide.

Open, Shut Them

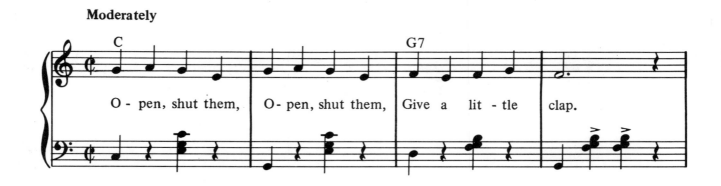

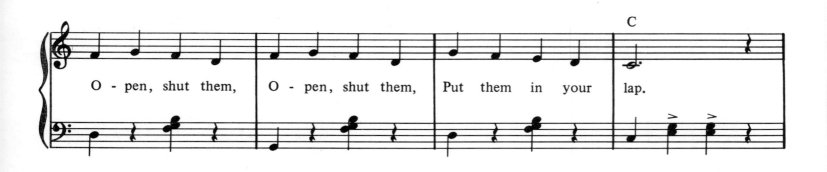

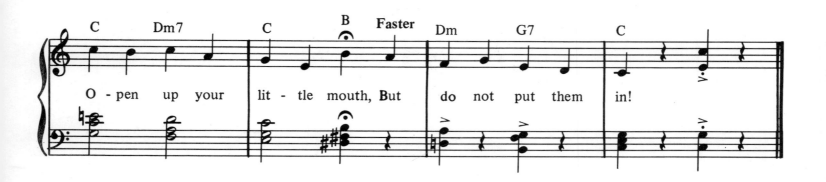

Hey Diddle Diddle

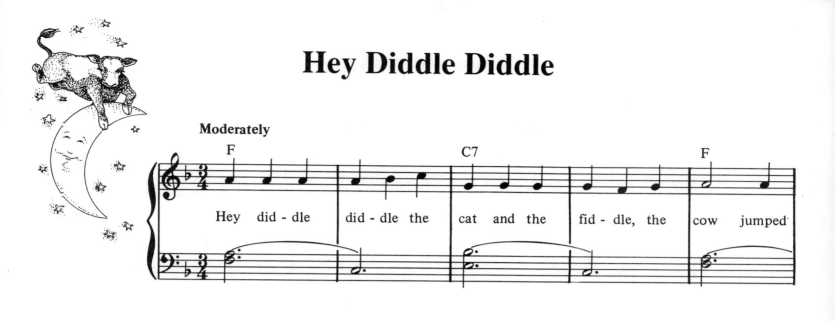

Moderately

F		C7		F

Hey did - dle | did - dle the | cat and the | fid - dle, the | cow jumped

	C7		Bb	C7

o - ver the | moon. _____ | | The | lit - tle dog | laughed __ to

F	Dm	Gm	C7	F

see such | fun and the | dish ran a - | way with the | spoon. _____

19

This Old Man
Nick-Nack Paddywhack

Merry walking tempo

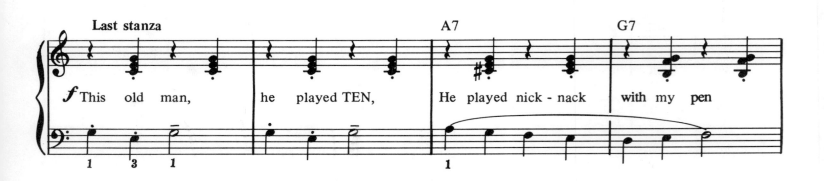

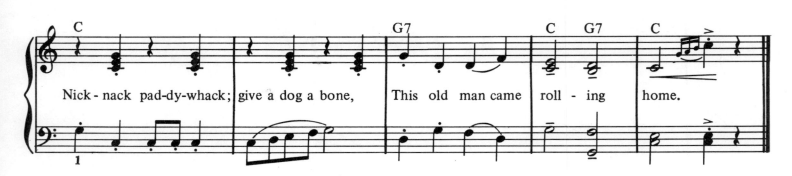

Make up your own rhymes for the successive numbers.

Zulu War Chant

Froggie Went A-Courtin'

Lively

1. Oh, Frog-gie went a-court-in', and he did ride. a-huh, a-huh.

Frog-gie went a-court-in' and he did ride,

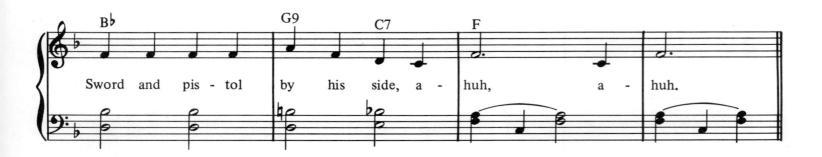

Sword and pis-tol by his side, a-huh, a-huh.

2. Well, he rode down to Miss Mouse's door, a-huh, a-huh,
   Well, he rode down to Miss Mouse's door,
   Where he had often been before, a-huh, a-huh.

3. He took Miss Mousie on his knee, *etc.*
   Said, "Miss Mousie will you marry me?" *etc.*

4. "I'll have to ask my Uncle Rat."
   "See what he will say to that."

5. Well, Uncle Rat rode off to town,
   To buy his niece a wedding gown.

6. "Where will the wedding supper be?"
   "Way down yonder in a hollow tree."

7. "What will the wedding supper be?"
   "A fried mosquito and a roasted flea."

8. First come in were two little ants,
   Fixing around to have a dance.

9. Next come in was a bumblebee,
   Bouncing a fiddle on his knee.

10. And next to come in was a big tomcat,
    He swallowed the frog and the mouse and the rat.

11. They all went sailing on the lake,
    And they all got swallowed by a big black snake.

12. There's bread and cheese upon the shelf,
    If you want any more, just sing it yourself.

Two Little Birds

Finger Game

Moderately

mf Two lit - tle birds sat on a hill; One named Jack and

one named Jill. Fly a - way Jack, Fly a - way Jill,

Come back Jack, Come back Jill.

London Bridge

Lavender's Blue

Head and Shoulders

Moderate march tempo

(Lyrics under the music:)

f Head and shoul-ders, **knees** and toes, knees and toes, Head and shoul-ders, kness and

toes, **knees** and toes,___ And ___ eyes and ears and

mouth__ and__ nose, head and shoul-ders, **knees** and toes, **knees** and toes.

While singing this song, quickly touch each part of the body as you sing about it. The movement is quite rapid, and it is challenging and fun to keep up with the words.

Once the song is known well, try this version: Sing the entire song, but each time the word "head" appears, don't sing it out loud, just touch your head. On the next repeat, leave out "head," and also leave out singing "shoulders" while you touch them. Keep adding one more silent gesture each time you repeat the song, until all the words have been eliminated and all that remains is rhythmic movement!

Hand Clapping Song

Chiapanecas

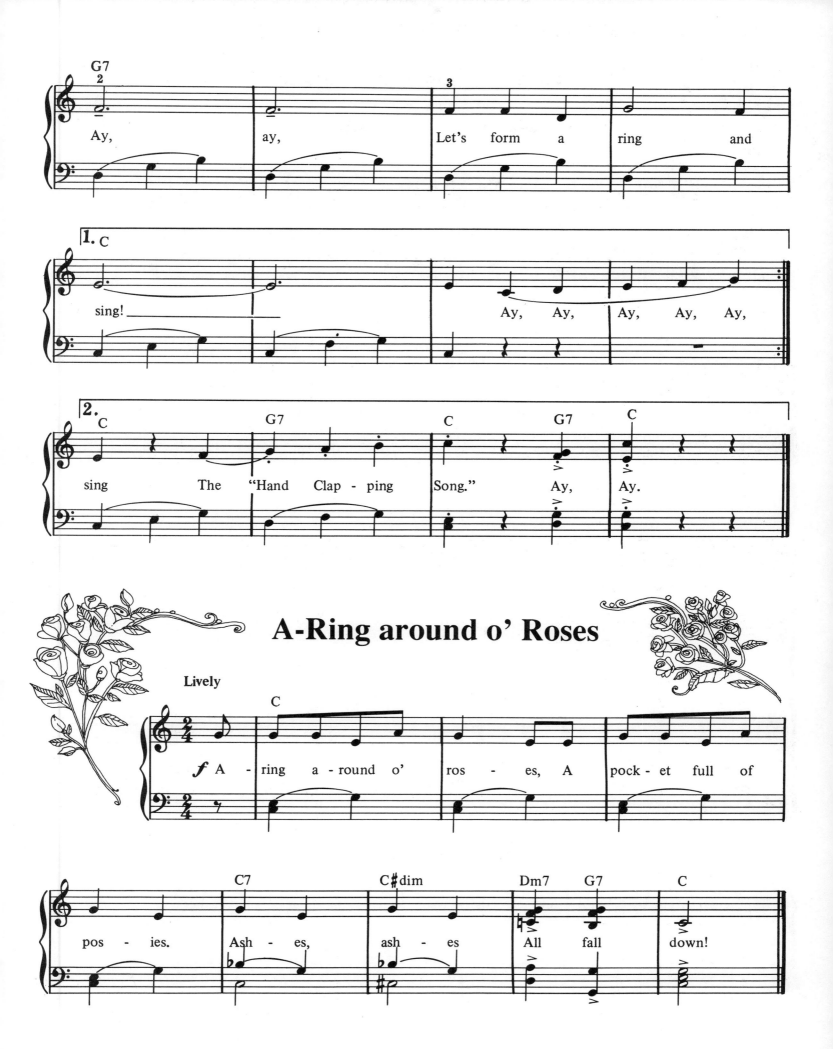

A-Ring around o' Roses

Eentsy-Weentsy Spider

Comfortably

The een-tsy ween-tsy spi - der went up the wa - ter spout;

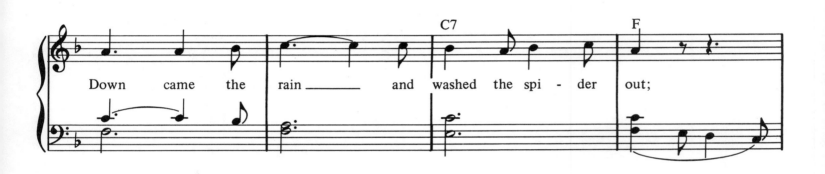

Down came the rain _____ and washed the spi - der out;

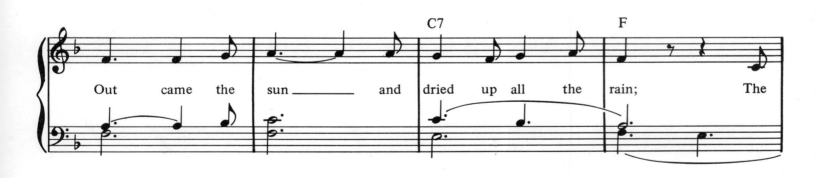

Out came the sun _____ and dried up all the rain; The

een - tsy ween - tsy spi - der went up the spout a - gain.

Finger Play

The eentsy-weentsy spider went up the waterspout;
Down came the rain and washed the spider out;

Out came the sun and dried up all the rain;
The eentsy-weentsy spider went up the spout again.

Spread out spidery fingers, creep up in the air.
Fingers "twinkle" raindrops as hands come back down.
Spread arms out wide, like the rays of the sun.
Repeat the first creeping motion.

Mary Had a Little Lamb

Moderately

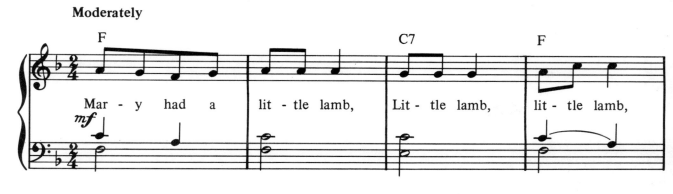

Mar - y had a lit - tle lamb, Lit - tle lamb, lit - tle lamb,

Mar - y had a lit - tle lamb, Its fleece was white as snow.

2. Everywhere that Mary went,
 Mary went, Mary went,
 Everywhere that Mary went
 That lamb was sure to go.

Pat-A-Cake

Lilting motion

This song is usually done with a partner. Start by holding up your forearms in front of you, with palms open, ready to clap in time to the song. There are two claps to a measure: (1) clap both hands with your partner; (2) clap your own hands together. Keep alternating these two clapping motions for the remainder of the song.

You can also make up other clapping patterns involving both hands, right hands, left hands, and so on.

30

Old MacDonald

Brightly

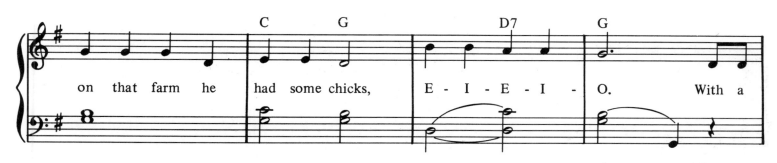

1. Old Mac-Don-ald had a farm, E-I-E-I-O. And

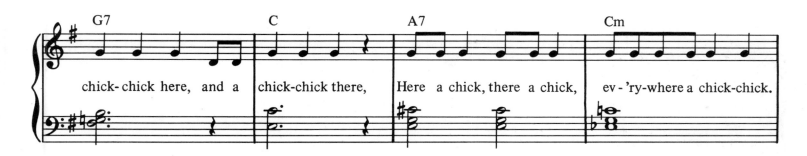

on that farm he had some chicks, E-I-E-I-O. With a

chick-chick here, and a chick-chick there, Here a chick, there a chick, ev-'ry-where a chick-chick.

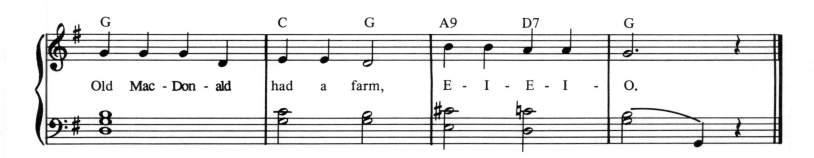

Old Mac-Don-ald had a farm, E-I-E-I-O.

2. Old MacDonald had a farm,
    E-I-E-I-O.
And on that farm he had some ducks,
    E-I-E-I-O.
With a quack-quack here, and a quack-quack there,
Here a quack, there a quack, everywhere a quack-quack.
Old MacDonald had a farm,
    E-I-E-I-O.

3. ...pigs, *etc.*
    ...oink-oink *etc.*

4. cows,
   moo-moo

5. turkeys,
   gobble-gobble

6. sheep,
   baa-baa

31

Pick a Bale o' Cotton
Jump Down, Turn Around

Reuben and Rachel

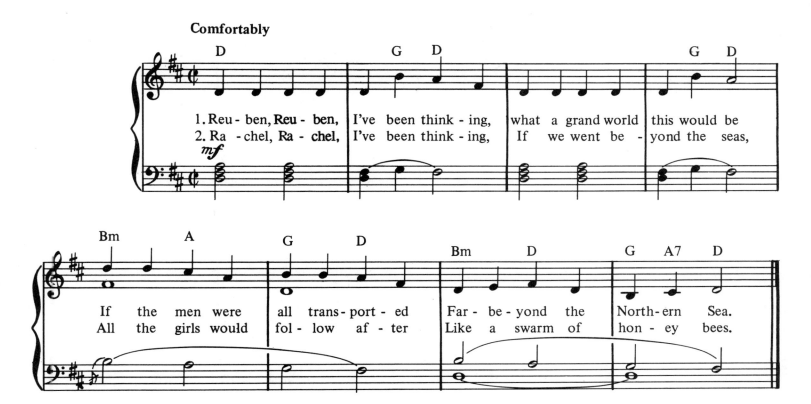

This song may be sung as a two-part round. The second voice enters at the second measure.

Love Somebody

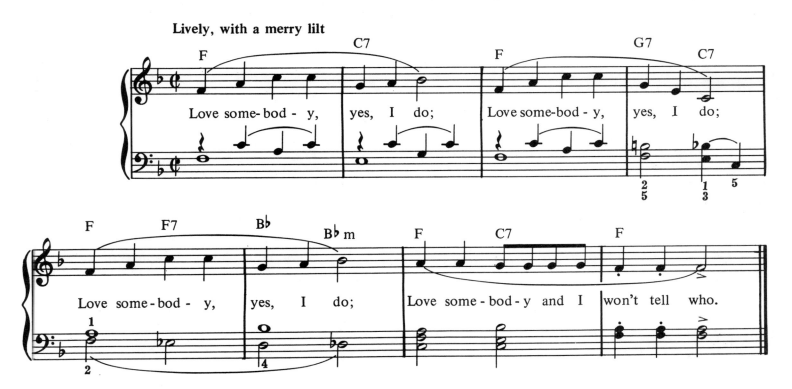

Five Little Chickadees

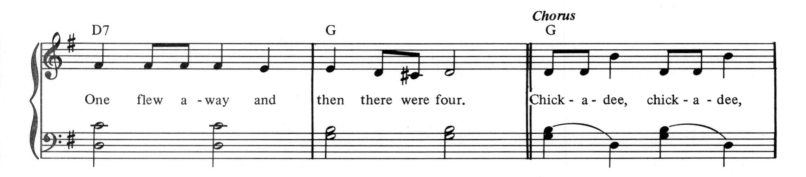

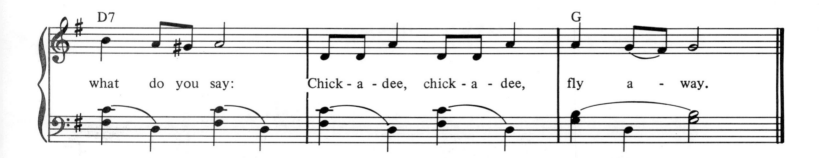

2. Four little chickadees sitting on a tree,
   One flew away and then there were three.

Chorus:

   Chickadee, chickadee, what do you say?
   Chickadee, chickadee, fly away.

3. Three little chickadees sitting in the zoo,
   One flew away and then there were two.

   Chorus

4. Two little chickadees sitting in the sun,
   One flew away ant then there was one.

   Chorus

5. One little chickadee sitting all alone,
   He flew away and then there were none.

   Chorus

This one works well with a group of children, having several fly away (running with flapping arm-wings) each time you sing the chorus. However, with even one youngster, it's fun to "finger play" and act it out.

verse

Five little chickadees sitting on the floor,

One flew away and then there were four.

Hold up one hand, showing all five fingers.

Hold up one hand, tucking under your thumb, showing four fingers.

chorus

Chickadee, chickadee, what do you say?

Chickadee, chickadee, fly away.

Spread your "wings" and tiptoe; fly around the room.

Repeat the finger play activity as you sing the verses, showing the right amount of fingers to go with the words. When you get to: ". . . and then there were none,"

Make an "all gone" gesture with open arms, or make a "zero" gesture with thumb and first finger.

For an added challenge, each time the chickadee flies away, tell him/her to get back to you on the last word of the chorus. It's not easy at first, but with some practice can be done!

Skip to My Lou

2. Flies in the buttermilk, shoo-shoo-shoo, *(three times)*
   Skip to my Lou, my darling.

Paper of Pins

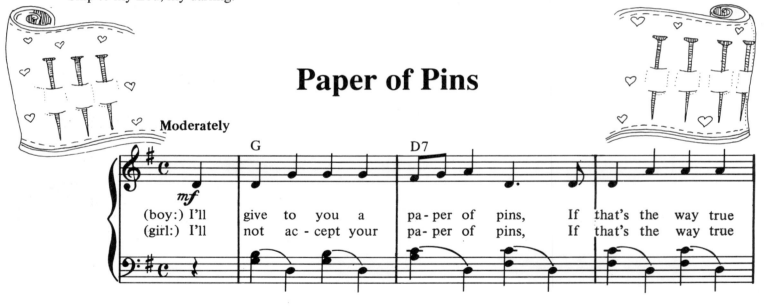

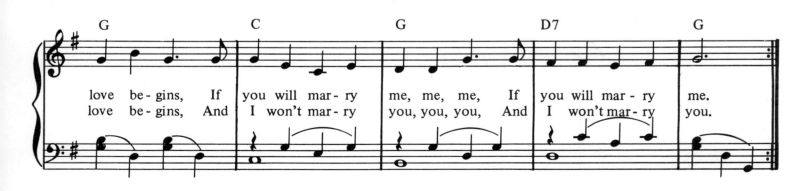

The Blue Tail Fly

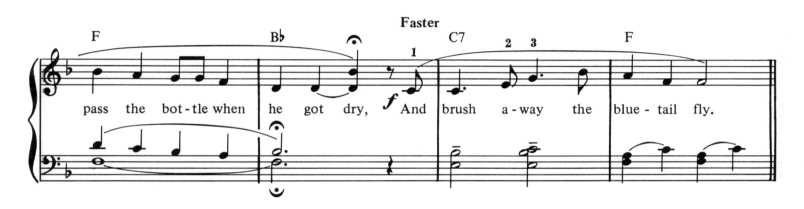

I've Been Workin' on the Railroad

Get out your hammer for this one, and get ready for some hard work! Hold your hammer up in the air, and bring it down hard (twice to each measure) as you sing.

I've been work-in' on the rail - road All the live- long day,

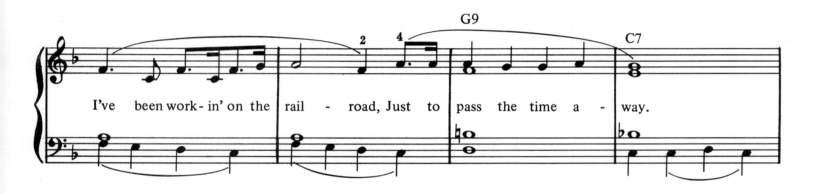

I've been work- in' on the rail - road, Just to pass the time a - way.

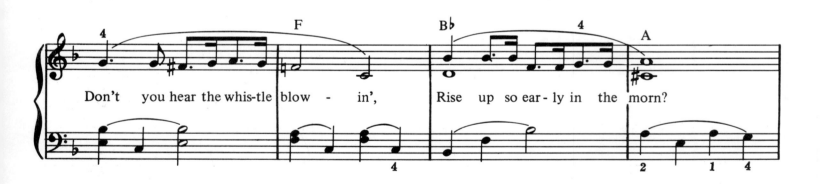

Don't you hear the whis-tle blow - in', Rise up so ear-ly in the morn?

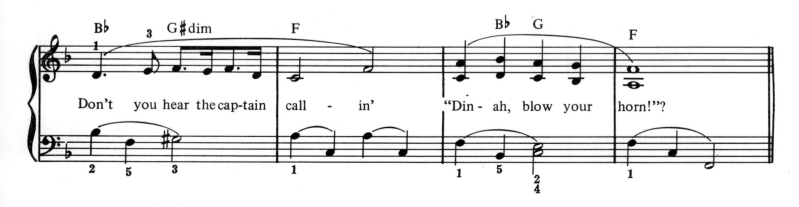

Don't you hear the cap-tain call - in' "Din - ah, blow your horn!"?

Bring a cupped hand to your lips and "blow your horn."

Din - ah, won't you blow,
Din - ah, won't you blow,
Din - ah, won't you blow your horn.

horn.(toot-toot)
Some-one's in the kitch-en with Din - ah,
Some-one's in the kitch-en I

"Strum the banjo" (four to each measure).

know,
Some-one's in the kitch-en with Din - ah,
Strum-min' on the old ban -

jo; and sing-ing:
Fee - fi - fidd-lee-i - o,
Fee - fi - fidd-lee-i - o

Fee - fi - fidd-lee-i - o,
Strum-min' on the old ban - jo.

rit.   *a tempo*

Fiddle-De-Dee

The Wheels on the Bus

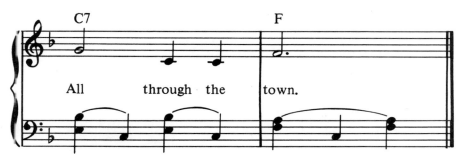

2. The horn on the bus goes beep-beep-beep,
   Beep-beep-beep, beep-beep-beep.
   The horn on the bus goes beep-beep-beep,
   All through the town.

3. The wipers on the bus go swish-swish-swish, *etc.*

4. The babies on the bus go waah-waah-waah,

While singing this song, you may rotate your forearms in front of you, imitating the motion of the wheels in time to the music. Then sing it again, this time faster, making your arms go faster also. Then try it again, this time much slower.

The Grand Old Duke of York

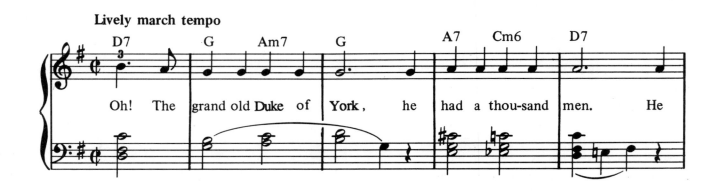

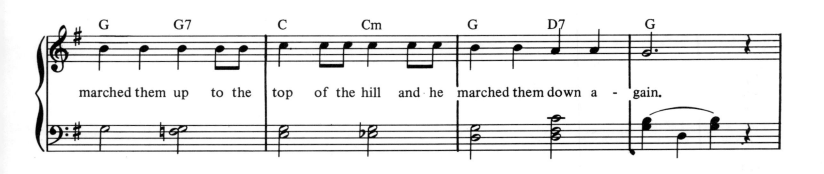

Oh! The grand old Duke of York, he had a thou-sand men. He
marched them up to the top of the hill and he marched them down a - gain.

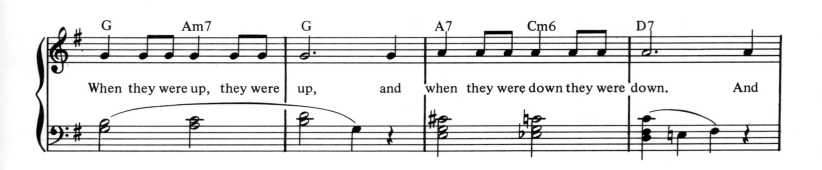

When they were up, they were up, and when they were down they were down. And

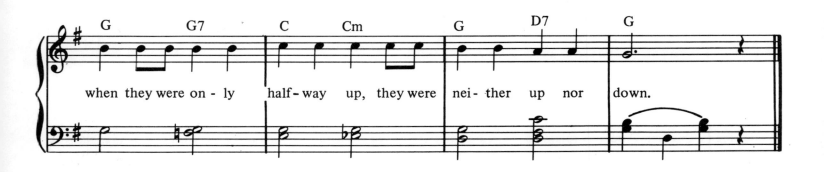

when they were on - ly half-way up, they were nei - ther up nor down.

Sing the song and act it out with gestures.

Oh! The grand old Duke of York,	*hands on hips*
he had ten thousand men.	*hold up hands, spread fingers*
He marched them up to the top of the hill	*march in place, up on toes, arms overhead*
and he marched them down again.	*march in place, gradually crouch down*
When they were up, they were up,	*jump up, arms raised*
and when they were down, they were down	*drop down, crouched*
And when they were only halfway up,	*stand, arms straight out*
they were neither up...	*jump up*
nor down.	*drop down*

Oh Where Has My Little Dog Gone?

Moderately

mf

Oh where, oh where has my lit - tle dog gone, Oh

where, oh where can he be? _____ With his ears cut

short and his tail cut long, Oh where, oh where___ is

he? _____

Little Jack Horner

Moderately

said, "What a good boy am I!"____

Over the River and through the Woods

Brightly

O - ver the riv - er and through the woods, To grand - fa - ther's house we

go; _____ The horse knows the way to car - ry the sleigh, Thro' the white and drift - ed

snow. _____ O - ver the riv - er and thro' the woods, Oh how the wind does

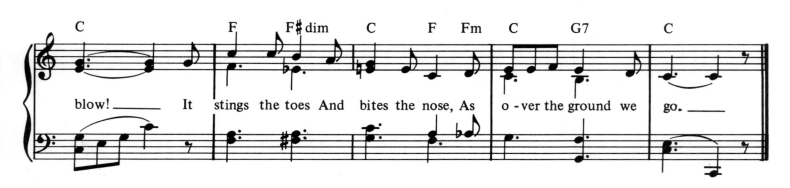

blow! _____ It stings the toes And bites the nose, As o - ver the ground we go. _____

Humpty Dumpty

Moderately

Bb / F9 / Bb Eb F7 / Bb

Hump - ty Dump - ty sat on a wall.

F9 / Bb C7 F7 / Bb

Hump - ty Dump - ty had a great fall. All the king's

F9 / Bb Eb F Gm Bb+ Bb / Cm

hors - es and all the king's men Could - n't put Hump - ty to -

F7 Eb F7 / Bb

geth - er a - gain.

Oh Dear! What Can the Matter Be?

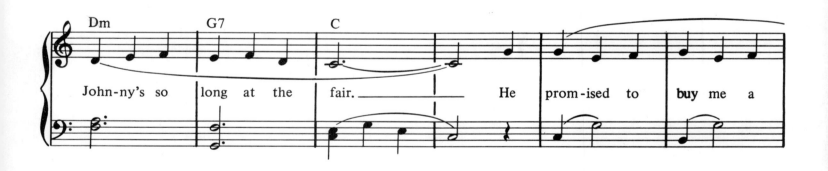

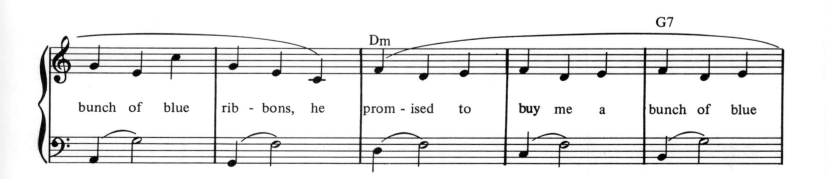

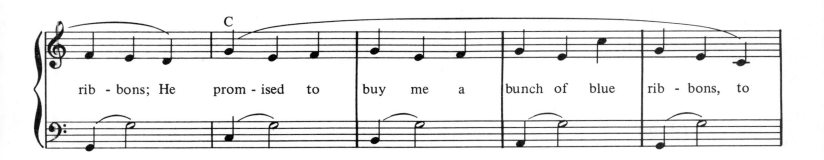

rib - bons; He prom - ised to buy me a bunch of blue rib - bons, to

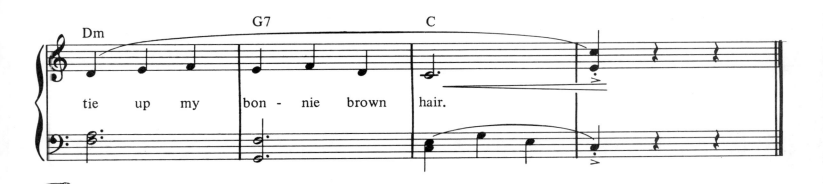

tie up my bon - nie brown hair.

The Farmer in the Dell

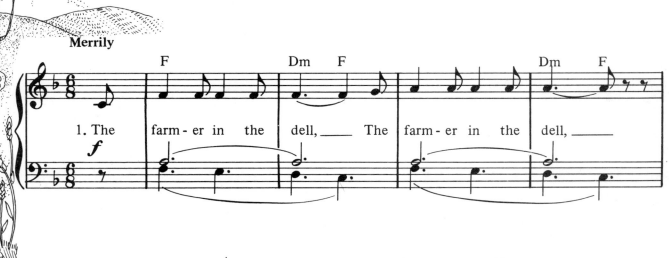

Merrily

1. The farm - er in the dell,____ The farm - er in the dell,____

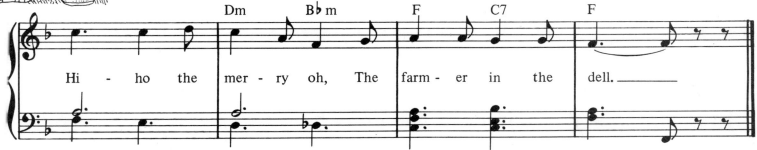

Hi - ho the mer - ry oh, The farm - er in the dell.____

2. The farmer takes a wife,
   The farmer takes a wife,
Hi-ho the merry oh,
   The farmer takes a wife.

3. The wife takes a child, *etc.*

4. The child takes a dog,

5. The dog takes a bone,

Row, Row, Row Your Boat
Round

Lively

Row, row, row your boat, gent - ly down the stream, Mer - ri - ly, mer - ri - ly, mer - ri - ly, mer - ri - ly, life is but a dream.

This song lends itself very well to movement. Sitting on the floor, simulate rowing movement, with your arms pulling the oars, leaning forwards and backwards as you row in time to the song. Then, sing the song faster, making smaller movements. Then try it slowly, with huge, exaggerated motions. It is also fun to move with a partner. For that game, sit cross-legged, opposite each other, close enough to hold hands while moving forward and back.

Row,   *pull back (on the oars)*
row,   *push forward*
row your   *pull*
boat,   *push*
gently   *pull*
down the   *push*
stream   *pull*
———   *push*

etc.

Alouette

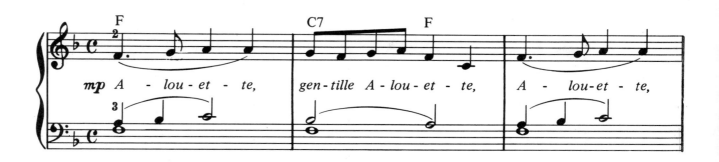

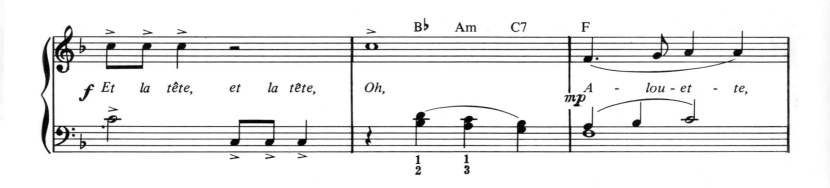

Billy Boy

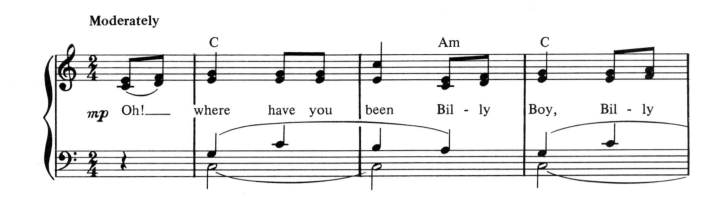

Polly, Put the Kettle On

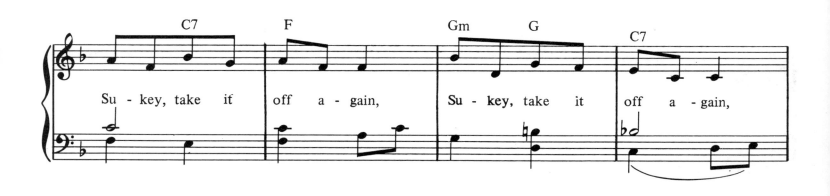

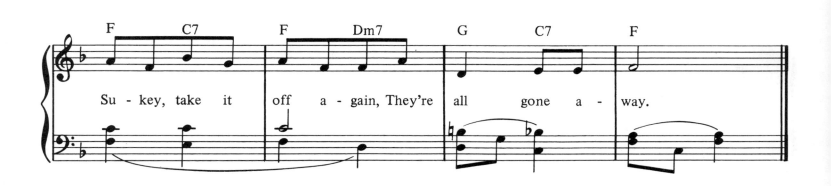

The Animal Fair

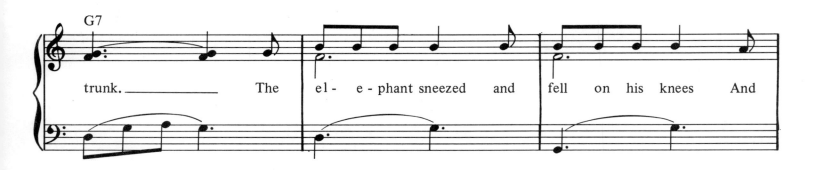

Hush, Little Baby

Moderately slow

1. Hush, lit - tle ba - by don't say a word, Ma-ma's gon-na buy you a

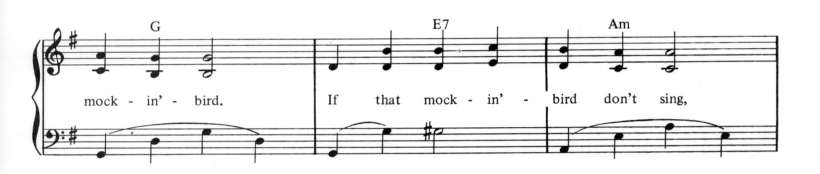

mock - in' - bird. If that mock - in' - bird don't sing,

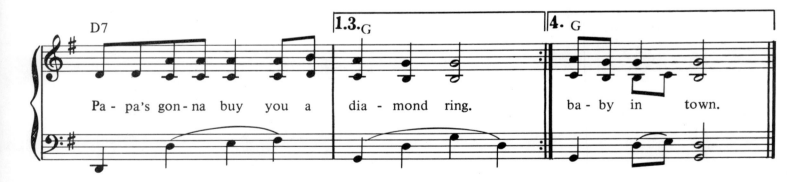

Pa - pa's gon-na buy you a dia - mond ring.

1.3. baby in town. **4.**

2. If that ring is made of brass,
   Mama's gonna buy you a lookin' glass.
   If that lookin' glass gets broke,
   Papa's gonna buy you a billy goat.

3. If that billy goat don't pull,
   Mama's gonna buy you a cart and bull.
   If that cart and bull turn over,
   Papa's gonna buy you a dog named Rover.

4. If that dog named Rover don't bark,
   Mama's gonna buy you a horse and cart.
   And if that horse and cart fall down,
   You'll still be the sweetest little baby in town.

The Bear Went over the Mountain

For He's a Jolly Good Fellow

The Monkeys Have No Tails in Zamboanga

Zamboanga is a town in the Philippines where American soldiers were stationed during World War II.

2. Oh, the monkeys have no hair in Zamboanga; *(two times)*
    Oh, the monkeys have no hair,
    Holy Smoke! but they are bare!
    Oh, the monkeys have no hair in Zamboanga.

3. Oh, the lions they are tame in Zamboanga;
    Oh the lions they are tame,
    But avoid them, just the same,
    Oh, the lions they are tame in Zamboanga.

4. Oh, we won't go back to Subic anymore;
    Oh, we won't go back to Subic,
    The mosquitos there are too big,
    Oh, we won't go back to Subic anymore.

No Ice Cream Today!

5. There's no ice cream in Manila, me-oh-my!
    There's no ice cream in Manila,
    Neither chocolate, nor vanilla,
    There's no ice cream in Manila, me-oh-my!

The Paul Bunyan Song

Words by Edna Lewis

Music by Denes Agay

Moderate, firm walking tempo

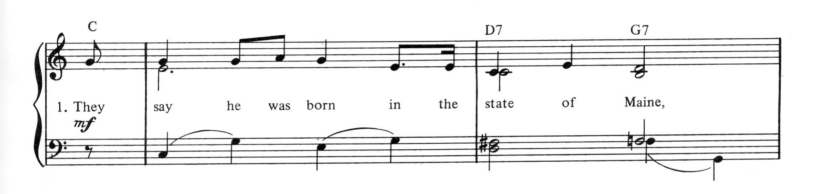

1. They say he was born in the state of Maine,

Strong-er than Sam - son big-ger of frame, Us - ing bare hands to up -

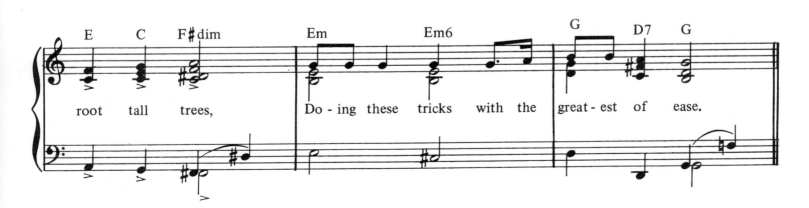

root tall trees, Do - ing these tricks with the great - est of ease.

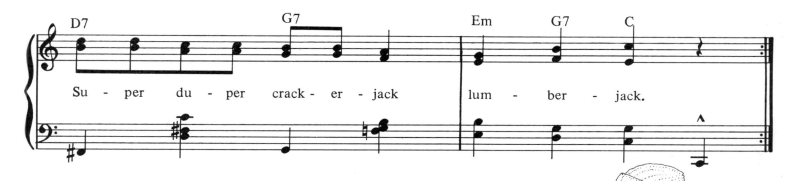

2. He was so quick when he shot a bear,
    He'd reach the spot 'fore the shot got there.
    His axe was made of a big oak tree,
    'Twas he who invented the lumber industry.

Chorus:

    Paul Bunyan, Paul Bunyan,
    Super duper crackerjack lumberjack.
    Paul Bunyan, Paul Bunyan,
    Super duper crackerjack lumberjack.

3. He found a blue calf in a blizzard one night,
    Taught him to work and do what was right.
    Some people say that the story is true:
    They dug the Great Lakes and Grand Canyon, too.

Chorus

Rockaby Baby

Effie J. Crockett

Gently swaying

Rock - a - by, ba - by, on the tree - top.

When the wind blows, the cra - dle will rock; When the bough

breaks the cra - dle will fall, And down will come ba - by,

Optional ending

cra - dle and all.

cra - dle and all.

With optional ending: Curl up on a chair, pretending to either rock in a cradle or lie asleep while listening to the song. At the end, at the *glissando,* "fall out" of the tree and crumple to the floor (gently, of course!).

Pop! Goes the Weasel

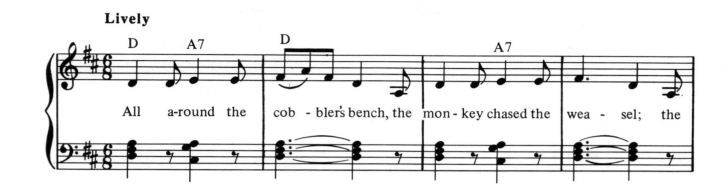

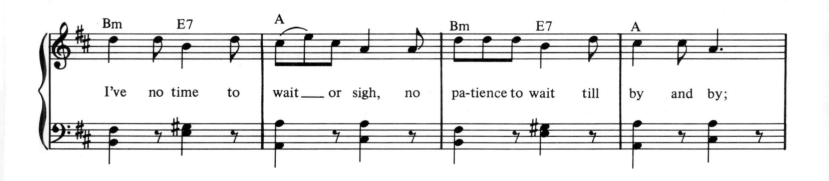

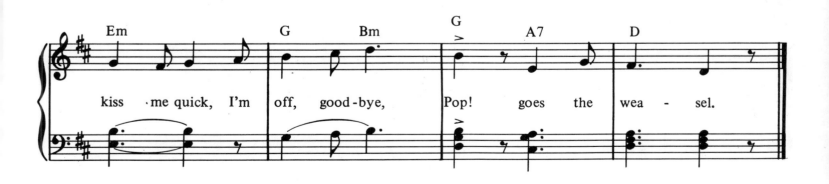

Oh! Susanna

Stephen Foster

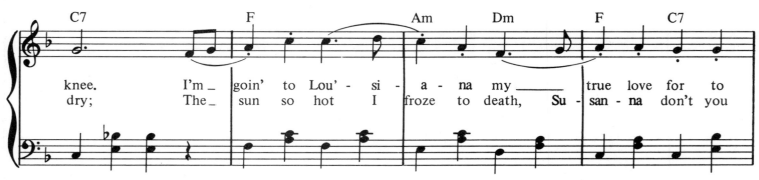

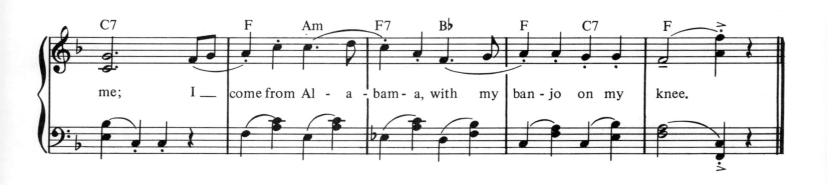

Yankee Doodle

65

There's a Little Wheel A-Turnin' in My Heart

2. There's a little song a-singin' in my heart,
    There's a little song a-singin' in my heart,
In my heart, in my heart,
    There's a little song a-singin' in my heart.

3. Oh, I feel so very happy in my heart, *etc.*

My Bonnie

Kookaburra

Round

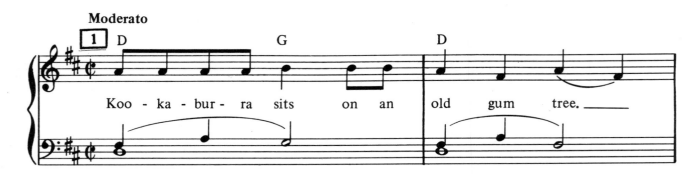

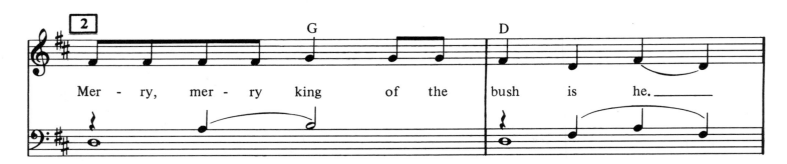

Koo - ka - bur - ra sits on an old gum tree. _____

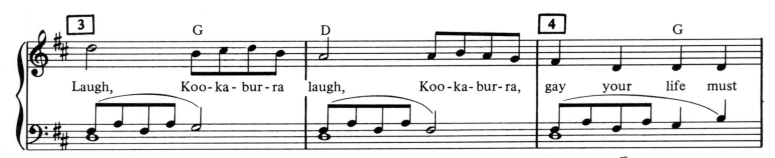

Mer - ry, mer - ry king of the bush is he. _____

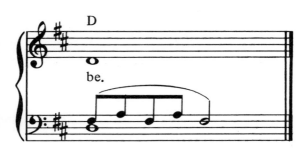

Laugh, Koo - ka - bur - ra laugh, Koo - ka - bur - ra, gay your life must

be.

First, sing the song "as is." Then, instead of singing the word "laugh" each time it appears in the song, it's fun to actually laugh instead! So, it is a good idea to first explore as many ways to laugh as you can; you might:

ha-ha-ha,
tee-hee-hee,
giggle like you are being tickled,
and so on.

The kookaburra *is a bird native to Australia. It has a gurgling call which makes it sound as if it is laughing.*

A Fly and a Flea

Moderately (with clear diction)

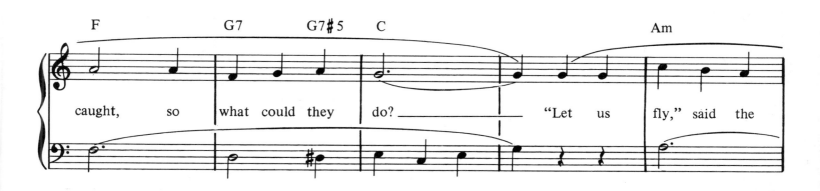

A fly and a flea in a flue ___ Were

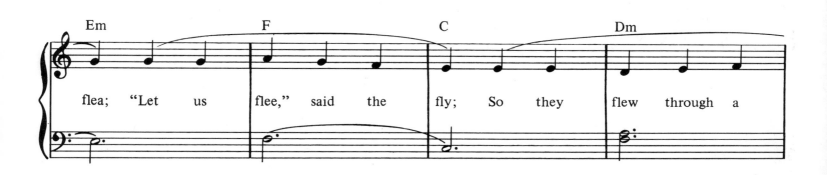

caught, so what could they do? ___ "Let us fly," said the

flea; "Let us flee," said the fly; So they flew through a

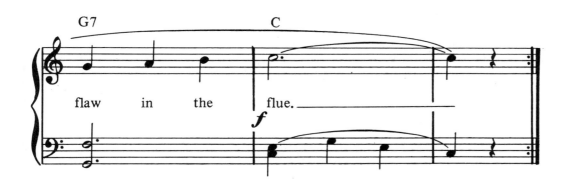

flaw in the flue. ___

Repeat this song a few times, singing faster and faster each time.

Monkey on a String

Words by Fred Wise

Music by Denes Agay

grand. _____ Though mon-keys in the zoo just play all day, it's true, he has no time for mon-key bus'-ness he has work to do. _____ When the hur-dy-gur-dy starts to play you'll join the crowd and get in-to the swing, Oh, ev-'ry-bod-y loves that mon-key on a string. _____

Three Blind Mice

Here is a fun way to act out this familiar song.

Three blind mice, three blind mice,
See how they run, see how they run.
They all ran after the farmer's wife,
    who cut off their tails with a carving knife,

Did you ever see such a thing in your life
    as three blind mice?

Shut your eyes tight.
Let your fingers do the running.
One hand chases the other.
Make a sharp chopping gesture with the side of
one hand.
Open your eyes as wide as you can.
Shut your eyes tight.

Oats, Peas, Beans and Barley Grow

I Am the Very Model

from The Pirates of Penzance

Words by William S. Gilbert

Music by Sir Arthur Sullivan

Brightly

Themes from "Peter and the Wolf"

Words by Jean Reynolds Davis

Music by Serge Prokofiev

Peter's Theme

Moderato

Oh, what a hap - py day, A day to chase all

cares a - way; I'll walk in the mead - ow and find a

friend. But grand - pa says. "No, no, no! The mead-ow's not a

place to go! There might be a wolf and you'd meet your end!"

The Cat's Theme
Grazioso

p Said the cat, "There's a bird, I will pes - ter her; ____ I'll grab her wing and make her sing, and then I'll run" ____ Pe - ter cried, "Lit - tle bird, hur - ry fly a - way; ____ That cat will tease and then tor - ment you just for fun!"

The Wolf's Theme
Moderato

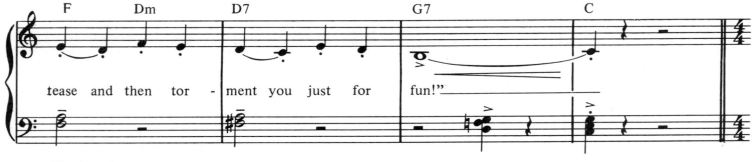

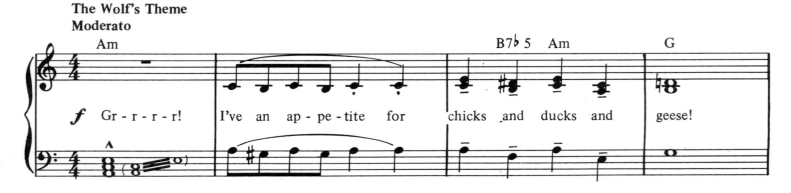

f Gr - r - r - r! I've an ap - pe -tite for chicks and ducks and geese!

76

The Hunters' Theme
Andante con moto

Themes from "The Mikado"

Words by William S. Gilbert

Music by Sir Arthur Sullivan

Lively

My ob-ject all sub-lime——— I shall a-chieve in time,——— To let the pun-ish-ment fit the crime, The pun-ish-ment fit the crime;——— And make each pris-'ner pent——— Un-will-ing-ly rep-re-sent——— A source of in-no-cent mer-ri-ment, Of in-no-cent mer-ri-ment!———

Lively

If that is so, Sing der-ry down der-ry! It's ev-i-dent ver-y, Our tastes are one. A-way we'll go, And mer-ri-ly mar-ry, Nor tar-di-ly tar-ry Till day is done.

Brother, Come and Dance with Me

from the opera Hänsel und Gretel

Engelbert Humperdinck

Instead of "Brother," you may use any name you like.